ALL ABOUT

World

HISTORY

ALL ABOUT

World

HISTORY

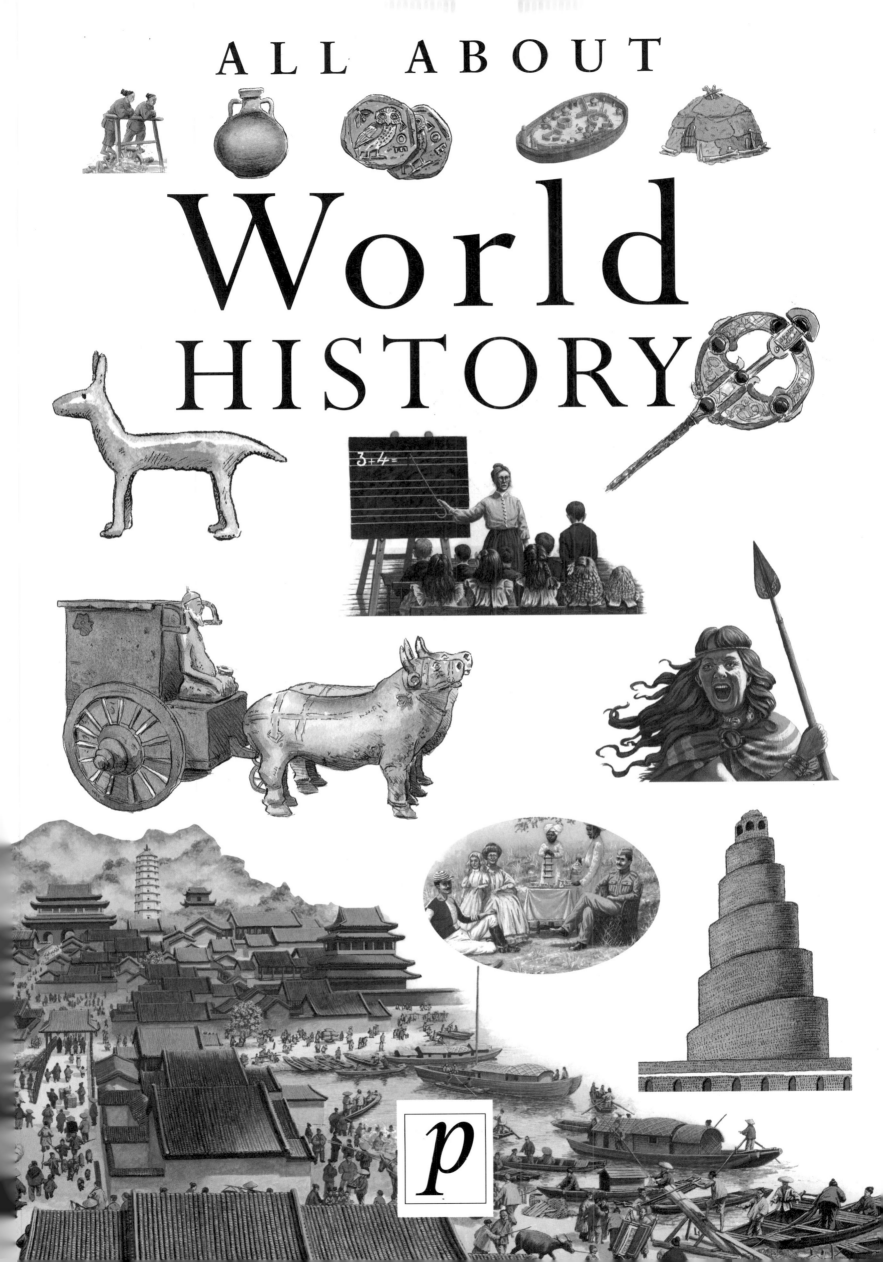

p

Author
Fiona Macdonald

Designers
Diane Clouting and Phil Kay

Editor
Linda Sonntag

Project Management
Raje Airey and Liz Dalby

Artwork Commissioning
Susanne Grant

Picture Research
Janice Bracken and Kate Miles

Additional editorial help from
Lesley Cartlidge, Jenni Cozens, Libbe Mella and Ian Paulyn

Editorial Director
Paula Borton

Art Director
Clare Sleven

Director
Jim Miles

This is a Parragon Book
This edition published in 2000
Parragon, Queen Street House, 4 Queen Street, Bath, BA1 1HE, UK
Copyright © Parragon 1999

Produced by Miles Kelly Publishing Ltd
Bardfield Centre, Great Bardfield, Essex, England CM7 4SL

ISBN 0-75253-600-1

Printed in Italy by G.E.P. Cremona

CONTENTS

HISTORY

ALL ABOUT HISTORY is divided into fifteen
different topics, each covered by a double
page spread. On every spread, you can
find some or all of the following:

- Main text to introduce the topic

- The main illustration, designed to inform
  about an important aspect of the topic

- Smaller illustrations with captions, to
  describe aspects of the topic in detail

- Photographs of unusual or specialized
  subjects

- Fact boxes and charts, containing
  interesting nuggets of information

- Biography boxes, about the people who
  have helped to shape the course of history

- Projects and activities

THE FIRST CIVILIZATIONS

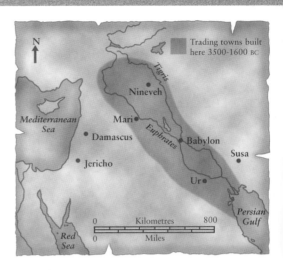

Trading towns built here 3500-1600 BC

TODAY'S MEN AND WOMEN are descended from ape-like creatures who lived in Africa about four million years ago. Unlike earlier apes, these creatures (known as Australopithicus, 'southern ape') walked upright. By 2.5 million years ago, their descendants (Homo habilis, 'handy man') had discovered how to make simple tools.

Hand-axes like this one made of flint were some of the world's earliest tools. They were invented by Homo erectus around two million years ago

Modern humans (Homo sapiens sapiens, 'wise man') first appeared about 100,000 years ago. They had large brains and used words to communicate, instead of signs and cries. By around 35,000 years ago, modern humans were living in Europe, Asia, and Australia; they migrated to America some time before 13000 BC. Early humans lived as hunters and gatherers, but some time around 9000 BC groups of men and women began to settle in villages and plant seeds of wild grains for food. This 'Agricultural Revolution' happened in the Middle East, but between 6000 and 3000 BC, farmers in Asia, America and Africa discovered how to grow rice, potatoes and yams. By around 7000 BC, the world's first towns had appeared.

Dating systems

Like many other history books, this encyclopedia uses a calendar that divides the past into two separate eras, BC (initials standing for before Christ) and AD ('Anno Domini', Latin words, orginally used by the Christian Church, that mean 'In the Year of our Lord'). According to this calendar, the year that Jesus Christ was born is counted as Year 1 AD. You count forwards from Year 1 in the AD era, and backwards from Year 1 in the BC era. There is no year zero.

The walls of Catal Hüyük houses were decorated with paintings; some have the skulls of oxen fixed to the wall. Dead people were buried under the floors

Houses in Catal Hüyük were built close together. The roofs were used as walkways, and the 'front doors' were in the roof

A ziggurat, a pyramid-shaped tower of mud-brick, stood at the centre of each Sumerian city.

The first towns

The first towns we know about were Catal Hüyük, in Turkey, and Jericho, in Israel. Both were at their biggest and strongest around 7000 to 6000 BC. They were surrounded by pounded earth ramparts covered with mud-plaster; inside, the houses were tightly packed together. The townspeople grew grain for food, but made most of their wealth through craft and trade. Farmers and hunters brought animals, furs and skins to towns, to exchange for craft goods such as pottery, jewellery, metalwork and cloth. Catal Hüyük (above) was a market centre for obsidian – a valuable black volcanic stone used to make knife blades. In early towns, people did not use coins; they had not yet been invented. Instead, they bartered (swapped) the goods they wanted to sell for other useful items. After around 6000 BC, these first towns became less important, as many new farming villages were built nearby.

SUMERIAN FACTS

- Sumerian kings were buried in huge 'death pits', together with their splendid furniture, jewellery, weapons – and many of their servants, who died alongside their royal masters.

- King Sargon of Akkad, a city to the north of Sumerian lands, was the first to unite the whole of Mesopotamia under one ruler, around 2300 BC.

- As well as inventing writing, the Sumerians also invented the wheel. But to begin with, they used it only for making pottery, not for transport.

Pyramids

Pyramids are massive monuments containing tombs. They were built in ancient Egypt, between 2686 and 1550 BC to house the bodies of dead pharaohs – the Egyptians' god–kings. The pyramids' shape was important. It represented the rays of the Sun. The Egyptians believed that dead pharaohs were carried to everlasting life in the land of the dead by the Sun's rays.

City life

Around 5000 BC, a group of people called the Sumerians arrived in Iraq. They settled in Mesopotamia – the land between the river Tigris and the river Euphrates. Grain, fruit and vegetables grew well there in irrigated fields. The Sumerians got rich by selling their farm produce to neighbouring peoples. Their population increased, and by around 3500 BC, their villages had developed into big, busy cities.

Making mummies

The Ancient Egyptians believed that people's spirits could only survive after death if their bodies survived as well. So they preserved dead bodies by removing the innards, drying the flesh and bones with chemicals, then wrapping the remains in bandages. Wealthy families also paid for fine painted mummy cases, or for stone caskets, called sarcophagi. Finished mummies were buried in tombs decorated with pictures of the dead person and their family enjoying life in the world of the dead. The word 'mummy' comes from the Arabic for bitumen (sticky black tar, found in the Egyptian desert). Mummified bodies often looked black and sticky because they were coated in resin – not tar, but scented gum from trees.

The Sumerians built ziggurats as homes for their gods. There was a temple at the top of each one

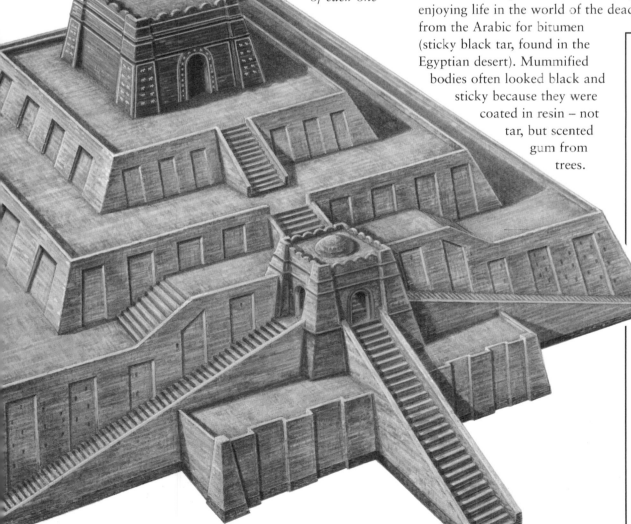

WRITE IN PICTURES

The first known writing system was invented by the Sumerians who lived in Mesopotamia around 3500 BC. It used picture-signs to represent objects, such as houses or birds or fish. Later, picture-signs were used to communicate ideas – the picture-sign for mouth (a pair of lips) could also mean 'speak'. Two picture signs could be combined to create a new meaning: for example, when written side by side, the signs for 'food' and 'mouth' meant 'eat'. Design some picture symbols of your own, and use them to write this message: 'I love learning about history.' (You can use a heart for 'love'.)

THE MEDITERRANEAN WORLD

FOR OVER 2,000 YEARS, the Greeks were the most powerful people in Mediterranean lands. From around 3000 BC, kings based on the island of Crete controlled Mediterranean sea routes, and demanded tributes from neighbouring lands. Around 2100 BC, new settlers arrived in Greek lands from the north and east. They set up powerful kingdoms ruled by warriors. Then, around 800 BC, Greece was divided into city-states. These were ruled by tyrants (strong men), oligarchs (groups of rich men) or, increasingly, by the citizens themselves. Over the centuries, a splendid Greek civilization developed. The Greeks were skilful designers, builders and craftworkers, and made many great discoveries in science, mathematics, medicine and philosophy. Greek writers also composed wonderful poems and plays. Greek power collapsed when the Romans invaded in 146 BC, but Greek ideas continued to flourish.

Great nations

Many other civilizations developed in the lands around the Mediterranean Sea, and in neighbouring Central Asia. Often, they fought one another, but they also formed close links through trade. The mighty Babylonian empire ruled Mesopotamia, and traded with India and Arabia. Further north, the warlike Assyrians were powerful from around 1100 to 612 BC. In 539 BC, another warlike people, the Persians, conquered the Babylonians. Persia also took over the nearby Greek colonies in Asia Minor, and the rich kindgom of Media on the shores of the Caspian Sea. The greatest trading nations were the Canaanites, who lived in present-day Syria, Lebanon and Jordan, from about 2000 to 1200 BC, and the Phoenicians who occupied the same lands after them.

The Hebrews

The Hebrews were nomads, who kept flocks of sheep and goats in eastern Mediterranean lands. Ancient stories, recorded in the Bible, tell how they were made to work as slaves in Egypt from around 1800 to 1200 BC. Led by Moses, a prophet or religious teacher, they escaped across the Red Sea and returned to their homeland. Around 1020 BC, they founded the nation of Israel, which was ruled by mighty kings. In 922 BC, Israel was divided in two; the southern part became known as Judah, and its inhabitants were called the Jews.

According to the Bible, Yahweh (God) gave the prophet Moses two slabs of stone with the Ten Commandments (holy laws for living a good life) written upon them

The Parthenon

The glittering white marble temple known as the Parthenon was dedicated to Athene, guardian goddess of the Greek city-state of Athens. It was built between 448 and 432 BC on top of the Acropolis, a high cliff-fortress in the centre of Athens, and was part of a grand rebuilding scheme planned by General Pericles (495–429 BC) after the Persians had invaded. Pericles was the leading Athenian statesman, who encouraged science, learning and the arts and wanted to make Athens the most beautiful city in Greece.

The Parthenon housed a gold and ivory statue of the goddess Athene. Every four years, the people of Athens held a ceremony to present the goddess with a new robe, called a peplos

The Olympic Games

The first recorded Olympic Games were held to honour the gods and took place in 776 BC, in southern Greece. To begin with, running was the only sport. Later, wrestling, boxing, horse-racing and chariot-racing were added, also pentathalon (wrestling, running, discus, long-jump and javelin), plus music, poetry and drama competitions.

King Nebuchadnezzar built the magnificent Hanging Gardens close to the royal palace in Babylon, and filled them with exotic plants and flowers to please his wife

Hoplites were armed with swords and spears, and protected by metal breastplates and helmets, leather greaves (leg-guards) and round shields. Each soldier had to buy his own weapons and armour

Babylon

Babylon was a rich city-state in Mesopotamia, to the north of Sumerian lands. It first became powerful around 1750 BC, when it was ruled by King Hammurabi, a famous lawgiver. The city had wide streets, rich palaces, huge ziggurats and temples, splendid gateways and massive walls. Babylon reached its greatest glory during the reign of the warrior king Nebuchadnezzar (605–562 BC).

Greek soldiers

Greek city-states were defended by armies of foot-soldiers, called hoplites. They were recruited from male citizens. In Athens, for example, young men aged 18 had to spend two years in army training. Only army commanders and rich citizens rode horses and chariots to war. On the battlefield, hoplites fought side by side in long lines (called phalanxes), holding out a wall of spears towards their advancing enemies.

Phoenician graves were decorated with extraordinary masks, like this one, made of pottery. They were probably meant to frighten evil spirits away

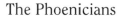

The Phoenicians

From around 1200, the Phoenicians lived in Canaan, at the eastern end of the Mediterranean. They were farmers and skilful craftworkers, making beautiful purple cloth and delicate glass. Phoenician scribes invented an early form of the alphabet we still use today. The Phoenicians were also expert sailors and shipbuilders, travelling to trade all round the Mediterranean Sea.

ALEXANDER THE GREAT

Alexander the Great (356–323 BC), king of Macedon, was a brave and brilliant army commander who had ambitions to rule the world. After conquering Greece and the mighty Persian empire, he led his army on a long march (about 30,000 km) across Central Asia to India and back. This journey took over 10 years, and helped spread Greek language, art and ideas over a very wide area. Alexander died of a fever aged only 33. His empire was divided among his generals after his death.

THE ROMAN EMPIRE

ORIGINALLY, THE ROMANS were farmers who lived in central Italy. Their neighbours were the powerful Etruscans. As the Romans grew stronger, they fought against the Etruscans, until around 753 BC they won control of the city of Rome. At first, the Romans were ruled by kings, but in 509 BC Rome became a republic, ruled by consuls – officials elected by the citizens. Senators, chosen from among top citizens, also helped shape government policy and make new laws. Over the years, the well-trained Roman army began to conquer more land, and by around 264 BC the Romans ruled all Italy. Soon, they controlled a vast empire overseas. In 47 BC, quarrels among power-hungry citizens led to a civil war. It ended in 27 BC, when an army commander, Octavian (later known as Augustus), took control. From then on, Rome was ruled by emperors. Some were wise and just – others were weak and cruel. Roman power finally collapsed in AD 476, after the city was attacked by tribesmen from Central Asia.

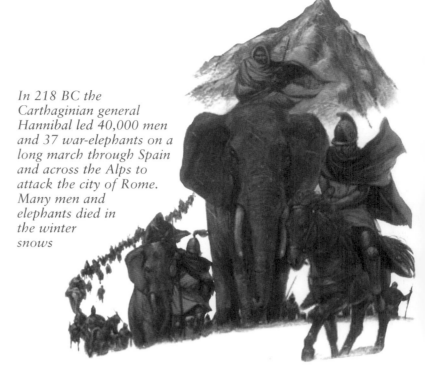

In 218 BC the Carthaginian general Hannibal led 40,000 men and 37 war-elephants on a long march through Spain and across the Alps to attack the city of Rome. Many men and elephants died in the winter snows

Carthage

In 814 BC, Phoenician traders founded the city of Carthage, on Africa's north coast. Carthage grew rich and powerful, and came into conflict with Rome. Between 264 and 146 BC Carthage fought and lost the three Punic Wars against the Romans. The Romans destroyed Carthage, and made all its citizens slaves.

The Romans as builders

The Romans were great builders and engineers. Rome was full of fine temples, palaces and monuments – and also aqueducts (to carry fresh water), public baths and sewers. Throughout the empire, Roman army engineers built roads, bridges and fortifications.

The city of Rome

Rome grew from a collection of farming villages around 750 BC to a city housing over one million people by AD 300. A survey made around that time listed 2 circuses (racetracks), 2 great arenas, 8 bridges, 28 libraries, 1,352 drinking-water fountains, 11 public baths, 144 public lavatories, 29 warehouses and over 46,000 private homes. There were also temples, forums (shopping centres) and government offices.

Rome was the centre of a vast network of international trade

Celtic gold necklace, shaped like a new moon

BOUDICCA

Boudicca was queen of the Iceni, a Celtic tribe who lived in southwestern England. A Roman writer described her as 'huge and frightening, with a mass of red hair that hung down to her knees. Her voice was as harsh as her looks.' After her husband, the king, was killed, she led a fierce rebellion against the Roman armies who wanted to control Iceni lands. Stories were told of how she led her army into battle herself, riding on a fast war-chariot. Boudicca's soldiers marched on the city of London, and set fire to it. But they were driven back by the Romans, and Boudicca herself was killed.

The Celts

The Celtic peoples of northwestern Europe were enemies of Rome. Celtic civilization first appeared around 750 BC in Austria but soon spread, through trade and migration, through France and northern Italy to Ireland, Britain and northern Spain. The Celts were farmers, warriors, poets, story-tellers and skilful craftworkers, making wonderful weapons and jewellery from bronze and iron. They fought fiercely against invading Roman armies. By around AD 200, Celtic civilization had disappeared from most of Europe.

Roman soldiers fought with spears, swords and daggers. To protect themselves, they wore padded leather helmets, metal or leather breastplates, and kilts made of strips of leather and metal. Underneath, they wore a wool or linen tunic, and (in cold climates) woollen socks and underpants. For the winter they had leather boots and a thick cloak

Roman soldiers

The Roman empire was guarded by large numbers of soldiers, recruited from citizens of the empire and from friendly lands. Recruits had to be fit, strong and under 25; they agreed to serve for long periods of up to 20 years and more. If they survived to retirement age, they were given a lump sum or a pension, and a 'diploma' recording their fighting years. On campaign, Roman soldiers lived in well-organized camps, or in semi-permanent forts – blocks of wooden buildings surrounded by earthworks and strong walls. An elite group of soldiers, called the Praetorian Guard, was created in AD 27 to protect the emperor and the city of Rome.

MAKE A ROMAN 'PIZZA'

Bread was one of the most important foods in Roman times. It was eaten at every meal. The Romans did not make modern-style pizzas – there were no tomatoes in Roman lands – but they did enjoy strong-tasting mixtures of onions, garlic and herbs with bread. They also liked olives, salty fish, sausages and cheese. You will need: a ready-made pizza base, 3 medium onions and 2 cloves of garlic, fried in oil, fresh or dried herbs, olive oil, olives, anchovies and tasty cheese.

Assemble the pizza and cook at 200°C for about 20 minutes. Serve with lettuce, a Roman favourite.

Rise and fall

By around AD 100, the Roman empire stretched from southern Germany to North Africa and the Middle East. Lands conquered by Rome were ruled by Roman governors, and guarded by the Roman army. Everyone living there had to pay taxes to Rome, and to obey Roman laws. In AD 395, the empire was divided into two parts, east and west. A new, eastern, capital city was built at Constantinople (present-day Istanbul).

MEDIEVAL EUROPE

IN WESTERN EUROPE, from around 800 to 1400, society was organized according to the feudal system. Almost everyone, from the greatest noble to the lowliest peasant, was bound by ties of loyalty and obedience to a superior lord. In return for performing duties for him, they were rewarded with food, money or, more usually, land. Their duties varied: peasants had to work on the lord's farms, nobles and knights (trained soldiers from noble families) were expected to fight by his side. European society was also shaped by another powerful organization – the Christian Church. Priests and monks were the best-educated people in medieval Europe; they played an important part in government, scholarship and the arts.

Barbarian invaders

From around AD 300, the Roman Empire was threatened by barbarian invaders. Vandals and Goths attacked from the north and west; Huns and Alans invaded from the east. In AD 410, barbarians set fire to the city of Rome. They were driven away, but returned. In AD 476, they forced the last Roman emperor to give up his throne. Europe was in chaos, but after AD 700, new kingdoms took shape, ruled by warrior kings like Charlemagne.

CHARLEMAGNE

Charlemagne (ruled AD 768–814) was king of the Franks, a warlike people who lived in southwestern Germany and France. He conquered a rich empire in Italy, Austria, Hungary and northern Germany, and on Christmas Day AD 800 was crowned Holy Roman Emperor by the Pope in Rome. Charlemagne was a great law-maker, and a patron of learning and the arts. He encouraged trade, repaired Europe's old Roman roads, and standardized the empire's system of weights, measures and coins.

Viking warriors fought with swords and battle-axes. Sometimes, they worked themselves up into a frenzy before battle, so they would fight extra fiercely. This was called 'going berserk'

The Vikings

The Vikings lived in the cold, harsh land of Scandinavia. They were skilful sailors and bloodthirsty pirate raiders, who brought death and destruction to many countries in northern Europe between AD 793 and 1100. But Viking people were also peaceful farmers, traders and craftworkers, who developed the world's first parliament and a system of strong laws.

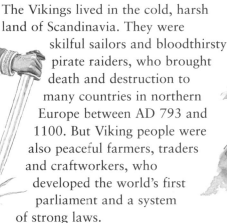

Freedom in the towns

The feudal system had very little effect on people who lived in towns. They made their living from craftwork, or by trade, and did not owe obedience to a lord. In AD 800, townspeople were a tiny minority of the European population. But towns grew in wealth and importance throughout the Middle Ages. Town councils built fine churches, cathedrals and council chambers; buyers and sellers from miles around hurried to weekly market days.

Medieval lords employed well-trained officials to run their estates and supervise the peasants who worked there

Castles

Castles were first built around AD 1000 as military strongholds. Later they became important family homes.

Living on the land

Most people in medieval Europe earned their living from the land. Peasant men, women and children laboured in the fields, ploughing, sowing and harvesting, making hay, picking grapes for wine, and making butter and cheese. Some peasants were not even free to leave their lord's farm.

Pilgrimages

In the Middle Ages, pilgrims made journeys to say prayers at Christian holy places throughout Europe and the Middle East. A pilgrimage had a serious purpose, but it could also be fun. Pilgrims stayed at inns to rest and refresh themselves, and to enjoy good food and ale. They travelled in groups for company, but also for protection against bandits and thieves.

Town houses were mostly built of wood, straw and plaster. They had thatched or tiled roofs. In busy cities, they were built tightly packed together. This often led to disastrous fires

The Black Death

The Black Death was a terrible epidemic (outbreak of disease) that arrived in Europe from Asia in 1347. The germs that caused it were carried in the blood of rats and fleas (mostly living in dirty, crowded towns) and passed on to humans by flea-bites. Medieval people did not understand this; they tried many different remedies, such as saying special prayers, washing in herb-scented vinegar, or carrying lucky charms. But none of them worked. The Black Death killed millions of people.

Spread of the Black Death

British Isles
1347
1348
Russia
Germany
France
EUROPE 1349
Spain
Italy
Greece
Turkey
AFRICA
ASIA
N
0 Kms 800
0 Miles 500

THE MUSLIM EMPIRE

THE PROPHET MUHAMMAD was a religious leader who lived in Arabia from AD 570 to 632. Muhammad taught people to worship Allah (God) and to live good lives. His teaching led to the growth of a major world religion, called Islam ('obedience to God'). It is still followed by millions of people today. In AD 622 Muhammad was forced by enemies to leave his home city, Mecca. He went to Medina, an Arabian market town, where he and his companions developed a new lifestyle, based on their faith. They became known as 'Muslims' – the people of Islam. Muhammad returned to Mecca with an army in AD 630, and captured it. Soon, Muslim soldiers took control of all Arabia, spreading their faith wherever they went. By AD 750 they had conquered a vast empire, stretching from southern Spain to the borders of China.

A great Muslim city

The Muslim lands were ruled by princes called caliphs, and governed by Muslim laws. At first, the caliphs' capital was at Medina, then at Damascus (in Syria), but they soon moved it to Baghdad, a magnificent new city (now in Iraq). Baghdad was founded by Caliph al-Mansur in AD 762. It was a circular city with a great mosque at the centre, and the caliph's palace nearby. Within the city walls there were schools, colleges, hospitals, bath-houses, libraries, gardens, fountains, markets, shops, and an observatory for studying the stars. In 1258, Baghdad was destroyed by invading Mongol armies.

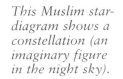

This Muslim star-diagram shows a constellation (an imaginary figure in the night sky).

Muslim science

Muslim rulers encouraged learning and Muslim scholars were skilled at medicine, mathematics, astronomy, philosophy and science. They got their knowledge from ancient Greek texts, which they translated into Arabic, the language used by scholars all over the Muslim world. They also made many important discoveries themselves. The numbers we use today (1, 2, 3 etc.) were developed by Muslim scholars around AD 850 from earlier Indian originals. We also use many Muslim scientific words, such as 'chemistry' and 'algebra'.

Decorating a mosque

Muslim artists were forbidden to portray people or animals (only God could create life). Instead, they decorated buildings with graceful patterns, based on mathematical shapes. They also used words from the Qur'an, the Muslim holy book.

Muslim engineers discovered how to build high curving domes above square or rectangular prayer-halls – no one else had been able to do this properly before.

Mecca

The city of Mecca, in Arabia, was an ancient holy site. After AD 630, when the Prophet Muhammad and his soldiers captured Mecca, it became the holiest place in the Muslim world and an important centre of pilgrimage. At the heart of the city stood the Kaaba ('cube'), a building housing a holy relic known as the Black Stone. Muhammad taught that the Jewish Prophet Abraham had worshipped God there, long ago. Today, Muslim people aim to make a pilgrimage to Mecca at least once in their lives.

Christian knights were soldiers from noble families who fought the Muslims on horseback. The Church taught that it was a knight's duty to protect the Christian faith.

The Crusades

The Crusades were wars fought between Christian and Muslim armies over who had the right to rule the city of Jerusalem (in present-day Israel) and the surrounding lands. This area was holy to Muslims, Christians and Jews. The Crusades began in 1096, when a Christian army set out for Jerusalem from Europe. They ended in 1291, when Muslim soldiers from Asia, North Africa and the Middle East drove the last Christian army out of the Holy Land.

Muslim Crusading armies (soldier, right) formed a tough, well-trained fighting force. Muslim army engineers invented siege engines and fire-bombs, and pioneered a useful way of sending messages from the battlefield, by pigeon post.

Muslim rulers issued fine gold and silver coins, decorated with Arabic writing. They were used by traders in many different Muslim lands.

GENGHIS KHAN

During the 13th century, the Muslim lands were conquered by fierce Mongol armies. The Mongols were nomads, who lived in central Asia. In 1206, all the Mongol tribes joined together under the leadership of a soldier prince called Temujin, and set off to conquer new lands. Temujin took the title 'Genghis Khan' (it means 'world ruler'). He united all the lands conquered by the Mongols into a mighty empire, made new laws and encouraged trade. When he died in 1227, he ruled all Asia, and half China, too.

Crafts and trade

Many important international trade routes passed through Muslim lands. Ships carrying spices, cotton cloth and precious stones from India, Africa and the East Indies arrived in the Persian Gulf and the Red Sea. Merchants led camel-trains across Asian mountains and deserts to bring silks from China. All these goods were sold in markets or bazaars (shopping centres) in Muslim lands, along with fine locally made craft goods, such as glass, pottery, metalwork and carpets.

Muslim scientists and engineers designed and constructed many beautiful buildings, especially mosques (buildings for worship), palaces and schools.

EARLY CHINA AND JAPAN

CHINESE PEOPLE CALLED THEIR NATION the 'Middle Kingdom'. They believed it was the centre of the world. From AD 618 to 1279, under the Tang and Song dynasties (families of emperors), China was one of the richest and most advanced civilizations on Earth. The Chinese built huge, splendid cities, and developed new and better varieties of rice. The population increased rapidly, and the army conquered large areas of land. Chinese scientists made many important inventions and discoveries, such as printing, paper-making, gunpowder, rockets and clockwork. Chinese craftworkers made silk cloth and porcelain (which we call 'china'), that were highly prized in Europe, Africa and Asia.

Neighbours

Japan and Korea were two of China's neighbours. Japan was ruled by emperors, who claimed to be descended from the gods. Ordinary people grew food in tiny garden plots, and caught many kinds of food from the sea. Korea was home to many famous scholars and scientists, and Korean craftworkers pioneered many pottery-making and ironworking techniques.

Chinese cities were administered by government officials. They collected taxes and made sure the laws were obeyed

The Great Wall of China

For centuries, China was divided into many separate states, which were often at war. In 221 BC, Prince Cheng from the state of Qin, conquered all the others and united them. He became China's first emperor, and reigned until 210 BC. Cheng was a formidable ruler. He imprisoned or killed all his enemies, burned books he did not agree with, passed new laws, built roads and canals, and introduced a new system of coins, weights and measures. He also rebuilt earlier, small-scale earthworks to create a huge Great Wall to defend his empire from enemy attack.

In warm South China and sheltered lowland Japan, rice grew very well. In cold North China and the Japanese mountains, wheat and barley were the usual crops

The emperor's palace was built of wood and decorated in bright red lacquer. Red and yellow were royal colours

Rice farming

Chinese and Japanese farmers grew rice in flooded paddy-fields. It was exhausting work. Each seedling had to be carefully planted by hand, and workers had to wade ankle-deep in mud to pull out weeds that might damage the crop. For extra food, Chinese and Japanese farmers bred fish in the flooded fields, and raised waterfowl, such as geese and ducks.

The Silk Road

Valuable goods made in China – especially silk cloth and porcelain (fine pottery) – were carried overland to Europe, North Africa and the Middle East along the 'Silk Road'. This was not a single pathway, but a series of rough tracks over 7,000 kilometres long leading across high mountains and treacherous deserts. It took merchants many months to travel from one end to another. Bandits, lack of food, and bad weather made the journey very dangerous at times. Along the way, travellers rested in 'khans', or boarding houses.

Samurai fought with swords, bows and arrows, and were expert horse-riders. They wore strong but lightweight armour, made of leather and wicker (woven bamboo). Their helmets were often decorated with splendid crests

Faith and worship

The Buddhist faith originated in India around 500 BC. It taught that people will only ever achieve peace and calm if they learn not to be ruled by selfish desires. Buddhism was introduced to Japan by monks and scribes from China and Korea around AD 550. The Japanese emperors and their courtiers all decided to follow this new faith.

Temples were made of carved and painted wood. Unlike most other Japanese buildings, they might be several storeys high – a sign that they were special. Often, they contained huge statues of the Buddha – the founder of the Buddhist faith

War and peace

Samurai were elite Japanese fighting men, who served in private armies belonging to great 'daimyo' (warlords and landowners). They were meant to follow a strict code of conduct, called 'bushido' (the way of the warrior), which taught that it was nobler to die fighting than to surrender.

EARLY AMERICA

OVER 300 DIFFERENT NATIVE PEOPLES lived in North
America. Each people spoke their own language,
followed their own customs and made their own
laws. Their lifestyle depended on where they lived.
In the icy Arctic regions, Inuit hunters survived by
catching walrus and seals. On the grass-covered
Great Plains, the Sioux and the Comanche hunted
herds of buffalo. The Iroquois of the cold
northeastern forests grew corn and hunted deer. In
the harsh desert lands of the Great Basin, the
Paiute people lived as nomads, hunting rabbits and
gathering grubs, seeds and nuts. Native peoples of
South and Central America ruled several great
empires. The Olmecs, the Maya and the Aztecs
ruled in Mexico; the Nazca and the
powerful Incas reigned in Peru.

*This Aztec knife,
made of semi-
precious stone, was
used for killing
victims for sacrifice.*

Sacrifices to the gods

Many Meso-American civilizations, such as the Aztecs and the
Maya, practised human sacrifice. They killed prisoners captured
in war as offerings to the gods of the Sun, the rain and growing
plants. They believed that blood from the sacrificed captives would
feed the Sun, make the crops grow in the fields and encourage the
rains to fall.

Mesa Verde

The Anasazi people of
southwestern North America
managed to survive in hot, dry,
semi-desert lands. They dug
irrigation ditches to carry water
to their fields and built large
communal dwellings,
like this one at Mesa Verde
(Colorado), in the cool shelter
of overhanging cliffs.

CIVILIZATIONS
IN CENTRAL AMERICA:
Olmecs 1200 BC–400 BC
Early Maya 1000 BC–AD 300
Classic Maya AD 300–600
Zapotecs AD 300–900
Mixtecs AD 600–500
Toltecs AD 900–1200
Aztecs AD 1300–1530
IN ANDES MOUNTAINS:
Chavin and Paracas 900 BC–200 BC
Nazca 200 BC–AD 600
Mochica 100 BC–AD 700
Huari AD 600–900
Chimu AD 1000–1450
Incas AD 1420–1540

The Maya people

The Maya lived in Central America, in today's Mexico,
Guatemala and Belize. They were most powerful around
AD 200–900, though Maya states existed for centuries
afterwards, and many people still maintain Maya traditions
and languages today. Maya lands were divided into city-
states, each ruled by a warrior king who was honoured like
a god. Ordinary people grew maize and beans, raised
turkeys and kept bees, collected wild plants for food and
medicines and hunted for jaguar fu
skins and coloured feathers from
birds in the rainforest.

Moveable homes

Native American nomad peoples like the Blackfoot and the Dakota (Sioux) lived in moveable tipis (leather tents) when buffalo-hunting on the Great Plains. This vast area of grassland stretched from the Mississippi River to the Rocky Mountains. After around 1690 they hunted on horseback and used horse-power to move their tipis and follow the buffalo herds.

Totem pole

Tall totem poles, carved from the trunk of a single massive tree, were made by Native American peoples who lived in the rain forests along the Northwest American coast. They hunted bears and beaver, and caught salmon in rivers and streams. Each totem pole tells a family's history; it also portrays protective ancestor spirits and gods.

The Inca empire

This little statue of a llama (an animal related to deer) was made by the Inca people who lived in the high Andes mountains of Peru. The Incas relied on llamas to carry heavy loads – they had no wheeled transport – and to provide them with soft, warm hair, which they spun and wove to make clothes. For almost 100 years, from 1438 to 1532, the Incas ruled a mighty empire, including parts of present-day Colombia, Bolivia and Chile. Under Inca rule, everyone in the empire was given work to do – growing food like maize and potatoes, working at crafts, building roads or fighting in the army.

Maya kings and queens were buried in magnificent pyramid-shaped temples, decorated with carvings and glyphs (picture symbols).

Maya learning

The Maya were the first Americans to invent a system of writing and keep detailed records. They used glyphs (picture symbols) written in codexes (folding books) to describe important events, myths and legends, and the achievements of their kings. The Maya were also expert astronomers and mathematicians, using just three numbers (1, 5 and 0) to perform complicated calculations, and to predict the movements of stars and planets in the night sky. They developed two very accurate calendars, one for farmers and government officials, with 360 days, and another, for priests religious scholars, containing 260 days.

Religious wars

In 16th- and 17th-century Europe, many people quarrelled about religion. Campaigners, known as 'Protestants', broke away from the Roman Catholic Church to set up new churches of their own. They disagreed with Roman Catholic beliefs, wanted to worship in their own languages, and to decide how their local churches were run. For over 150 years, between around 1500 and 1650, Europe was torn apart by bitter religious wars. They were fought between rulers and peoples who supported the rival Protestant and Roman Catholic branches of the Christian faith.

Exploring the world

In 1419, explorers from Portugal began to sail along the west coast of Africa. It was the start of 200 years of pioneering voyages in ocean-going wind-powered ships. These voyages had dramatic consequences. For the first time, Europeans and peoples from America, India, Southeast Asia and the Far East came into regular contact; sometimes they worked peacefully together, sometimes they fought.

EUROPEAN UPHEAVALS

THE 16TH AND 17TH CENTURIES were a time of rapid change throughout Europe. There were upheavals in religion and government, and in ideas about art and science. New inventions like printing and new information about the rest of the world brought back by explorers raised questions in many people's minds. These were exciting, but disturbing, too. People no longer agreed about how they should live and worship. Some, like the Mayflower settlers, left home to set up new communities in distant lands. Others began to question how their countries should be run. Most rulers held fast to traditional beliefs. But in some countries, terrible poverty and economic problems led to calls for government reform.

IMPORTS

Explorers' pioneer voyages also led to an enormous increase in international trade between 1600 and 1800. Many plants, such as tomatoes and potatoes, and animals from America were introduced to Europe and Asia. In return, Asian plants like sugar and African plants like coffee were carried to America, where they were grown on plantations worked by slaves.

Magellan's crew sailed in a battered second-hand cargo-vessel called the Vittoria. It became the first-ever ship to sail round the world

After Columbus's Atlantic voyage in 1492, explorers from Europe pioneered new sea routes and set out to conquer the world

Renaissance

The word 'Renaissance' is used to describe the period from around 1400 to 1600. It was an exciting time when new ideas in art, architecture, science and learning flourished in many European lands. The Renaissance began in Italy. Many of the greatest Renaissance artists, such as Michaelangelo (who painted this chapel ceiling), lived there.

Thirty Years' War

One of the worst religious conflicts was the Thirty Years' War (1618–48), between Austria and Spain (Catholics) and some German states, Denmark and Sweden (Protestants). Spain and Austria ruled parts of Germany, and wanted to ban the Protestant faith from their lands. The war caused dreadful damage and terrible loss of life. No one could 'win', but when it ended, the German states were given freedom to worship as they chose.

Civil War

King Charles I of England believed he had a divine (God-given) right to rule. Many of his people did not agree, and this led to a civil war (1642–8). Parliament won, and King Charles was executed. England became a republic, and an army commander, called Oliver Cromwell, ruled England as 'Lord Protector'. He, in turn, was replaced by the King's son, who ruled as Charles II.

PUMPKIN SOUP

Pumpkins were one of the vegetables that Native American people helped the Mayflower settlers grow after they landed on the eastern coast of North America. Today, American people eat pumpkins on Thanksgiving Day (the last Thursday in November), a national holiday held each year to remember a special meal cooked by the settlers in 1621. The settlers wanted to give thanks to God for a plentiful harvest which provided them with stocks of food to last through the coming winter. To make a nourishing pumpkin soup, you will need: 500 g pumpkin flesh, 1 large onion, 2 medium potatoes, 2 large carrots, 2 sticks celery, 1 small red pepper. Chop all the vegetables and cook very gently in oil. Add 500 ml water and simmer until soft. Whizz the vegetables in a blender until they  make a pulp. Add enough milk to make a thickish soup. Heat through, stirring all the while. Serve with bread and cheese.

Pilgrims

In 1620, a group of 102 men, women and children with strong Christian beliefs decided to leave England for far-away America, where they could set up a new community, run their own church, and make their own laws, based on the Bible. They sailed in a cramped, leaky ship called the Mayflower, and endured a long, stormy voyage across the Atlantic Ocean. They landed (in Massachussetts) as a bitter winter began. Over half of them died; the rest only survived because friendly Native American people gave them food and showed them how to grow American crops like pumpkins and maize. The next year, 1621, they managed to gather a plentiful harvest which gave them food for the winter and made them safe.

Ever since 1799, when an American writer invented the name, the religious pioneers who sailed in the Mayflower have been called the 'Pilgrims' – people who made a long, dangerous journey because of their faith

PETER THE GREAT

Peter the Great became Tsar (emperor) of Russia in 1689, when he was 17 years old. He had ambitious plans to modernize Russia. He introduced new skills and techniques in navigation and shipbuilding, copied from western Europe. He encouraged Russian exploration into Siberia, and founded a new capital city, called St Petersburg, on the Baltic Sea coast. But his rough, brutal behaviour made him very unpopular. He died in 1725.

EARLY AFRICA

FOR OVER 1,000 YEARS, rich, powerful kingdoms flourished in many parts of Africa. They mostly owed their wealth to trade. African workers discovered how to mine precious metals, such as gold and copper, and also emeralds and other precious stones. Products from magnificent African animals, such as elephant ivory and rhinoceros horn, were also highly prized in many other lands. The African rulers who controlled this trade used their wealth to pay for many fine buildings and works of art, and to support strong, well-trained armies to defend their lands. Many peoples in Africa followed ancient traditional religions, but, after around AD 800, kingdoms in North and West Africa became converted to Islam.

This Nok terracotta sculpture shows a man with a decorated hairstyle. He may be a priest or a king.

The Nok

The Nok people lived beside the mighty Niger River in West Africa. They were at their most powerful between around 800 BC and AD 200. The Nok were farmers, metalworkers and potters, who made huge, sometimes lifesize, figures out of terracotta (baked clay). These statues portray people (left), as well as wild and domesticated animals. They were probably made for religious purposes.

Between 1200 and 1300, ten Christian churches were cut out of the solid rock in the kingdom of Ethiopia, Northeast Africa. They were excavated by workmen using only simple mallets and chisels. It was an astonishing feat of construction. Most of the churches were shaped like crosses, the holy symbol of the Christian faith. They soon became great centres of pilgrimage.

Links with other lands

Africa is a vast continent, and travel overland from north to south or east to west was almost impossible at most times in the past. As a result, many regions of Africa were linked more closely to other countries and continents than they were to distant African lands. Most of these links were formed by sea travel. Ethiopians travelled to Arabia and Central Asia across the Red Sea, East African kingdoms bordered the Indian Ocean, and North African nations made contact with countries in Europe and the Middle East by sailing across the Mediterranean Sea.

The Kingdom of Axum

The kingdom of Axum, in Ethiopia, traded with Arabia, India and the Mediterranean lands. It exported many precious goods, including gold, ivory, precious stones, live monkeys, tortoiseshell and spices. Axum was ruled by all-powerful 'Kings of Kings', who paid for many wonderful buildings, including tall stone pillars and churches hewn from rocks. Axum was one of the first countries to become Christian, around AD 300.

Trade and wealth

Between around AD 700 and 1600, merchants from the rich Muslim lands of North Africa led camel-trains laden with salt on long journeys across the Sahara to trade with people living in the powerful West African kingdoms of Mali, Ghana and Songhay. In return, they carried back cargoes of gold, leather and slaves. West African rulers used this wealth from trade to build fine palaces, mosques, schools and universities in cities on the edge of the desert, such as Jenne and Timbuktu.

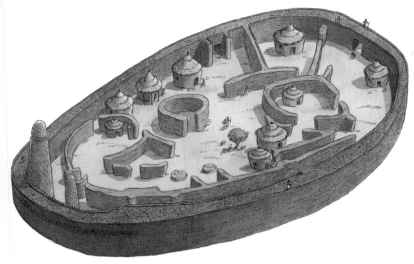

The Shona

The fortress-city of Great Zimbabwe was built for the Shona kings of East Africa, who ruled a powerful empire from around 1200 to 1600. Within its strong stone walls, Great Zimbabwe contained houses, palaces and tall stone towers for storing grain. The Shona people were farmers, who raised herds of cattle and planted crops of millet. They also mined iron, gold and copper, and hunted elephants for ivory. They traded all these goods at East African coastal ports. There, they met Arab merchants, who sailed to Africa across the Indian Ocean with precious cargoes of glass and perfumes from Arabia, jewels from India, and silks and porcelain from China.

The stones used to build Great Zimbabwe were carefully shaped and fitted by hand. No mortar was used to hold them together.

Camels were the only animals that could survive long enough without food and water to make exhausting journeys across the hot, dry desert, laden with valuable goods to sell. Their wide, flat feet did not sink into the desert sand, and they could store enough nourishment in their humps to last for about 10 days. Although camels were often smelly, stubborn and bad-tempered, they were highly prized.

North Africa

Rich, powerful dynasties ruled the fertile lands along the coast of North Africa (in present-day Morocco, Algeria and Tunisia). They built splendid cities, with fine palaces, libraries and mosques, and busy markets. Further inland, clans of nomad Berber people, called the Tuareg, managed to survive in the desert. They lived as nomadic herdsmen, keeping camels, sheep and goats and travelling across the desert from oasis to oasis in search of water.

Market towns grew up at oases along the edge of the Sahara desert, where people and animals had access to reliable water supplies.

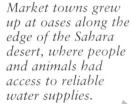

This beautifully decorated brass portrait head was made in the West African kingdom of Ife around 1200.

Artists and metalworkers

African artists were skilled at many crafts, especially stonework and metalwork. Between around 1200 and 1900, metalworkers living in the rainforest kingdoms of Ife and Benin (part of present-day Nigeria) made beautiful portrait statues and plaques (square picture-panels) of shiny golden metals called brass and bronze. The plaques were used to decorate the royal palace in Benin city; the portrait statues were placed on royal family altars to honour dead ancestors.

INDIA

OVER THE CENTURIES, the vast sub-continent of India has been home to many great civilizations. Some of the world's first cities were built by farming peoples who lived in the Indus Valley, in present-day India and Pakistan. They disappeared around 1500 BC, perhaps because their land was over-used, or because they were attacked by Indo-Aryan invaders. The Indo-Aryans introduced a new religion, called Hinduism. For years, India was divided into many small Hindu kingdoms, but by 322 BC, kings belonging to the Mauryan ruling family had conquered a large empire. The next great Indian empire was ruled by the Hindu Gupta dynasty, which came to power in AD 320. They encouraged science, learning and the arts. Hindu kings reigned in southern India for almost the next 1500 years, though they were often threatened by invaders, and sometimes fought among themselves.

The Muslims

In 1175, the first Muslim rulers came to power in India. They ruled kingdoms in the north and the west. Then, in 1526, India was invaded by Muslim warriors descended from the Mongol peoples of Central Asia. They became known as the 'Mughals', and, by 1600, had conquered most of India. The Mughals ruled India for more than three centuries. The first Mughal emperors were strong and warlike; they aimed to create a brilliant civilization by encouraging all that was best in India, regardless of social background, religion or race. But after around 1700, Mughal emperors gradually lost power. The last Mughal emperor was forced to give up his throne when the British government took control in 1858.

The picture shows the first Mughal emperor, Babur, who ruled from 1526 to 1530. He was a famous collector of books and paintings.

Court painters

The Mughal emperors encouraged the finest artists from India and the neighbouring lands to come and work at their courts. Mughal painters created exquisite miniature paintings in brilliant jewel-like colours. Some were portraits and scenes of royal life at court; others were carefully observed studies of plants and animals.

Cities of the Indus Valley

Around 40,000 people lived in Mohenjo-Daro and Harappa, the two largest cities in the Indus Valley, between 2500 and 1500 BC. Both cities were well planned, with wide streets, spacious houses, running water and drains. In the centre of each city was a huge fortress, built on an artificial mound, where the rulers lived. This striking stone statue (right) was made around 2000 BC, in Mohenjo-Daro. It probably portrays a priest-king.

The way of peace

Hindu King Ashoka ruled the Mauryan empire in India from 272 to 231 BC. He began life as a warrior, but became sickened by the violence of battle. He turned to Buddhism, seeking understanding by peaceful means. He paid for Buddhist holy laws to be carved on rocks thoughout India, and for many Buddhist monuments. This decorated gateway marks the entrance to the Great Stupa at Sanchi, a dome-shaped holy site.

Trade with the West

The first European ship to sail to India reached the Malabar (western) coast in 1498. After that, European merchants made regular voyages to India. They purchased valuable Indian spices, cotton cloth, drugs and dyestuffs to sell in Europe. In 1600, a group of leading British merchants set up the East India Company, to organize and protect long-distance trade. It became immensely rich and powerful, and had its own private army.

Indian ports, such as Surat, Madras and Calcutta became important centres of international trade. Merchants met there to arrange deals in enormous warehouses.

TIMELINE

- 2500–1500 BC Indus Valley civilization.
- 1500 BC Hindu civilization begins.
- 500 BC Buddhist faith develops.
- 330 BC Alexander the Great brings Greek ideas to India.
- AD 50 Kushan empire powerful.
- AD 320 Gupta dynasty powerful.
- AD 750 Three Empires era.
- 1175 First Muslim empires.
- 1526 Mughals conquer India.
- 1858 India becomes part of British Empire.
- 1947 India becomes independent; new nation of Pakistan created.

Magnificent Mughal architecture

Many people think that the Taj Mahal (above), near Agra, in India, is one of the most beautiful buildings in the world. It is made of gleaming white marble, decorated with delicate flower patterns made of semi-precious stones. It was built by Mughal emperor Shah Jahan (ruled 1627–1658) as a tomb for his wife, Mumtaz Mahal. She died giving birth to their fourteenth child.

TIPU SULTAN

Tipu's name meant 'Tiger'. He gave orders for this life-size model of a tiger killing an Englishman to be made for one of his palaces.

Hindu Tipu Sultan was ruler of the South Indian state of Mysore from 1782 to 1799. Like many other Indian rulers, he fought against the British, who were trying to take control of India. Tipu lost half his kingdom after invading a nearby state which was protected by Britain. He was killed fighting British soldiers who were besieging his lands.

The British in India

Britain took control of India after Indian soldiers working for the British East India Company rebelled in 1857. In the following years, many British government officials, doctors, engineers, tea-planters and estate managers went to live and work in India. Often, their families accompanied them. The British community in India lived sheltered, privileged lives, looked after by Indian servants. They became known as the 'British Raj' (ruling class).

Members of the British Raj continued to follow an upper-class British lifestyle in India.

European merchant ships were built with huge wide hulls, to carry the maximum amount of cargo. Because of the strong monsoon winds blowing across the Indian Ocean, they could make the long voyage from England to Europe only once or twice a year.

PACIFIC LANDS

THE PACIFIC OCEAN is the largest body of water on earth. It covers an astonishing 180 million square kilometres. For thousands of years, the islands of the Pacific were remote from the rest of the world, cut off by wild waves and stormy seas. But the people living there – the Aboriginals, Polynesians and Maoris – developed unique and well-adapted civilizations. They found ways of surviving in environments that were often difficult and even hostile. The Aboriginals of Australia lived as hunters and gatherers, eating animals, insects and grubs they had caught, and many wild roots, berries and seeds. The Polynesians and Maoris (Polynesian settlers in New Zealand) lived by fishing and farming. In warm Pacific islands, close to the Equator, they grew yams, bananas, breadfruit and coconuts, and kept pigs, dogs and chickens. In colder New Zealand, they planted sweet potatoes, gathered seaweed and shellfish, and caught whales, seals and fish from the seas around their islands.

Maori forts

Groups of Maori settlers in New Zealand often fought against each other. To protect their families, they built their villages on well-defended hilltop sites and surrounded them with walls made of strong wooden poles. The Maoris were expert woodworkers, and decorated their most important buildings with wood-carvings in elaborate swirling designs.

The Aboriginals

The Aboriginal people settled in Australia over 50,000 years ago. With great skill, they discovered how to live in Australia's harsh natural environments – coastal swamps, rainforests and deserts. They dug shallow wells to find underground water, and used tools such as digging sticks (for finding grubs and tubers underground) and grinding stones (for crushing seeds and grains). They made cloaks and tents from skins and furs, spun thread from pounded tree bark, and hollowed out tree-trunks to make canoes.

Australian Aboriginal hunters used spears and throwing sticks, called boomerangs, to hunt emu and kangaroo. They also used nets and traps to catch fish and birds

Easter Island

Some time between AD 1100 and 1450, the people who lived on remote Easter Island carved 600 strange stone heads almost 10 metres tall. The statues probably represented ancestors, gods or kings. But because the entire population of Easter Island died out soon after 1500, no one knows for sure! Historians also do not know why Easter Island became deserted. Possibly, an environmental disaster struck after the inhabitants had cut down all the trees for building and firewood.

Easter Islanders arranged their huge statues in rows, to make a very impressive monument, thought to have magical power

MAKE A 'SKELETON' PICTURE

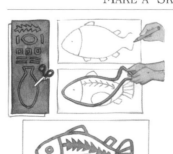

For many thousands of years, the Aboriginal people created paintings on cave walls in an amazing 'skeleton' style. Their artwork showed the bones and inner organs of different wild creatures, as well as the outer skins. They believed this way of painting helped them show the life-force and spirit of the animals they saw all around.

To make a skeleton picture, draw the outline of your animal on white paper. Trace the outline on to dark-coloured paper. Cut out the outline, then glue it on to the white paper. Cut out the shapes of bones, heart, lungs etc. in dark paper. Glue them on to the white paper. Decorate with paint or felt-tips.

IMPORTS

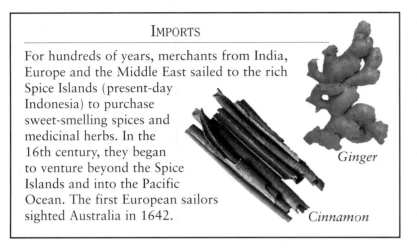

For hundreds of years, merchants from India, Europe and the Middle East sailed to the rich Spice Islands (present-day Indonesia) to purchase sweet-smelling spices and medicinal herbs. In the 16th century, they began to venture beyond the Spice Islands and into the Pacific Ocean. The first European sailors sighted Australia in 1642.

Ginger

Cinnamon

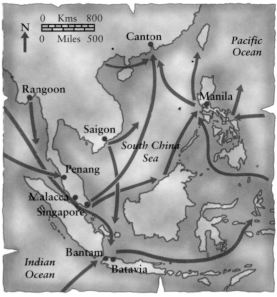

All ships travelling to the Spice Islands, or to China and Australia, had to pass through the narrow Malacca Straits. Rich trading towns grew up here and on the nearby islands, selling silks, spices and gems. After around 1500, they were conquered and ruled by European nations

Trading routes from Europe to the Spice Islands. After around 1850, many Chinese sailors, shopkeepers and farm labourers followed the Europeans to this area

The Maoris

The Maori people were very skilful sailors. The first Maori settlers made the long voyage across the Pacific to New Zealand from other Polynesian islands in wooden outrigger canoes. The largest ocean-going canoes might be over 30 metres long. They could carry up to 500 men, women and children, plus their animals, farm tools and seeds. They were pushed through the water by wooden paddles, or sometimes fitted with big triangular sails made of palm-leaf matting. Smaller canoes were also used by Maori fishermen, or by fierce Maori warriors on raids.

Australian settlers

It took nine months for sailing ships to travel from Europe to Australia. That was one of the main reasons why, in 1788, the British government decided to send convicted criminals there. Once in Australia, there was little chance that they would ever return to cause trouble! But Australia was a vast, exciting country which offered many opportunites, and before long the convict settlers were joined by willing migrants from Europe. Over 342,000 arrived between 1852 and 1861, some of the peak years for migration. Settlers hoped to make their fortunes as farmers, sheep-ranchers or gold-diggers.

AMERICA

ON 4 JULY 1776, a new nation was born – the United States of America. It consisted of only 13 states. They declared independence from Britain, which had ruled them as colonies for over 150 years. During the 19th century, the USA grew rapidly as more states joined the Union. Some were purchased from other European powers; some were conquered in wars. Some were given away in peace treaties, and others were simply taken over by pioneer farmers, who settled on uncultivated lands. American industry and business grew rapidly after oil, coal and steel were discovered in the northwest, and valuable gold in California. Millions of migrants arrived from Europe, hoping to make their fortunes in the 'land of the free'. By 1900, the USA was so successful that it was the richest country in the world.

Wagon train

From around 1850, many families left Europe and East Asia to make a new life in America. Some settled in cities along the east coast, others trekked westwards to reach the Great Plains, the Rocky Mountains and California. Settlers travelled in 'trains' of covered wagons, pulled by oxen or horses. During the long and dangerous journey, many died from hunger, thirst and disease, or in fights with Native Americans. Life in new western ranches, farms and mining settlements could be lonely and very hard.

The settlers and the Native Americans

When the first European settlers arrived in the 1540s, North America was home to around 300 different Native peoples. Sometimes, Native Americans and European settlers arranged to lived peacefully, side by side. They traded together, and occasionally helped one another with local information and offers of food. But more often, there were quarrels between them, because the European settlers felt they had a God-given right to take over Native peoples' lands. As more and more settlers arrived in America from Europe and Asia, these quarrels turned into war. The Native peoples fought bravely, but settler troops and settlers had bigger, better weapons, and drove most Native Americans from their homes. The last battle to defend Native peoples' land was fought in 1890 at Wounded Knee, South Dakota.

A replica of the Mayflower

Early migrants

The first Europeans to settle in America sailed there in ships like the Mayflower (a replica is shown right). In the 1540s, the Spanish settled in present-day Florida and California. In the 1580s, the French and English settled in present-day Virginia.

Railroad

Railways were vitally important in the new United States of America. By 1890, over 260,000 kilometres of track had been laid. They linked northern industrial cities and east-coast ports with the vast ranches and farmlands of the west and south. Building the railways was a great engineering achievement; lines had to be laid across mountains, deserts and swamps. In 1869, the first transcontinental railway line was completed. At a special ceremony the final sections of rail were joined together with a golden nail (left).

Northern (Unionist) soldier

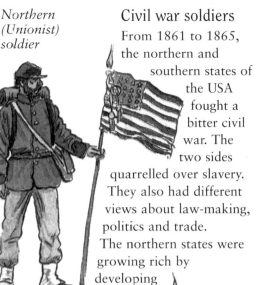

Civil war soldiers

From 1861 to 1865, the northern and southern states of the USA fought a bitter civil war. The two sides quarrelled over slavery. They also had different views about law-making, politics and trade. The northern states were growing rich by developing industry; in comparison, the southern states were poor farming country. Fighting lasted for four years. The northern states finally won, and slavery was outlawed throughout the USA.

Southern (Confederate) soldier

GEORGE WASHINGTON

Britain, France, Spain and Portugal claimed the right to rule the lands where Europeans had settled in North and South America. They also claimed the right to collect taxes there. The settlers thought both these claims were very unfair. In 1776, a group of 13 British colonies in North America decided to break away from British rule. The British sent soldiers to fight against the rebels, but were defeated in 1783. General George Washington (1732–99) led the American colonists in this War of Independence. In 1789, he became the first president of the USA.

Covered wagons were given the romantic name 'prairie schooners', because their canvas roofs, which billowed and flapped in the wind, reminded people of graceful sailing ships

Slavery

Since around 1500, black men, women and children from Africa were shipped to the Caribbean and to neighbouring regions of North and South America. They were sold to owners of plantations, huge estates where sugar and cotton were grown in very large quantities to be shipped back to the fast-growing towns and cities in Europe. The slaves had no freedom and no rights. They were often very cruelly treated, especially if they tried to run away. In 1807, Britain banned all her citizens from taking part in the slave trade anywhere in the world, and tried to encourage other European nations to ban slavery in the lands they ruled. But in the USA, slavery was not finally abolished until 1865.

INDUSTRIAL EUROPE

THE INDUSTRIAL REVOLUTION began around 1770 and lasted for almost 100 years. It was a time of rapid change in the way things were made. Engineers invented big machines to mass-produce goods quickly and cheaply in factories. At first, these new machines were only designed for spinning thread and weaving cloth, but they were soon used for making all kinds of useful things, such as shoes, paper, pottery and metal tools. They were also used to produce large quantities of strong materials for construction, ship-building and weapons production, such as bricks, iron and steel. The Industrial Revolution also brought many changes to the way people lived. Men, women and children working in huge factories replaced old-fashioned craftworkers, who used to make things at home, slowly and carefully by hand.

Railways

Railways helped the Industrial Revolution by carrying goods made in factories to shops and markets far away. They also carried fresh food from the countryside to feed families who worked in factory towns. The world's first passenger railway was opened by British inventor George Stephenson in 1825. Soon, railways were built in many parts of Europe.

Farm machinery

After around 1700, many people in Europe and America became fascinated by science. Farmers and estate-owners experimented with new ways of breeding animals and sowing crops. Alongside industrial scientists, they began to invent new machines to make farming quicker and more profitable. The seed drill (above) made a hole and planted a seed in one go.

Industrial towns

The first factories were built close to supplies of coal, iron-ore and water. These were necessary for making big new machines and providing power to run them. Often, they were found in the countryside, far away from existing towns. So, to provide housing for industrial workers, new towns were built next to the factories. Conditions there were often grim.

Mines

The owners of mines often employed children to work for them. They were very useful for crawling down tight tunnels, or squeezing in between huge machines. Many working children were killed in accidents with machinery, or died from illnesses caused by breathing coal dust, cotton fibres or chemical fumes.

Schools

In the early years of the Industrial Revolution, many children were forced to work long hours in dangerous conditions in factories and mines. But after around 1830, governments passed laws to protect child workers, and charities set up many more 'ragged' schools, where factory children could study after work and at weekends. By the 1870s, European governments began to set up state-funded schools, where pupils under 12 received free, compulsory education. By around 1900, most factory workers could read and write.

IMPORTED EMPIRE PRODUCE

Until the late 1800s, large parts of Africa, East Asia and Australia were cut off from the rest of the world. But, once European explorers had travelled across them, European nations hurried to seize rich, distant lands and claim them as part of their empires. Local people were not consulted. They found their lands ruled as colonies by far-away countries. European government officials, miners, ranchers, and farmers moved to live there and began to grow rich, exporting goods such as coffee beans back to their homelands.

KARL MARX

Karl Marx (1818–1883) was a German writer living in London. In 1848, he published a book called 'The Communist Manifesto'. In it, he demanded political freedom and better pay and working conditions for ordinary people. He called on workers to claim their rights: 'Workers of the world, unite! You have nothing to lose but your chains!'

After around 1800, thousands of poor, hungry, unemployed men and women migrated from the countryside to live in fast-growing factory towns. They hoped to find regular work and better pay. Wages in factories were better than those on farms, but working conditions in factories were often dirty and dangerous, and houses in factory towns were noisy, crowded and full of disease.

WARS & REVOLUTIONS

MORE THAN ANY OTHER TIME in history, the early 20th century was an age of wars and revolutions. In South Africa, from 1899 to 1902, Boer farmers (descended from Dutch settlers) rebelled against British colonial rule. In the Far East, a war broke out between Russia and Japan in 1904. Both wanted to be the strongest power in East Asia. The last Chinese emperor was forced to give up power by rebels who wanted a new, republican form of government which would give more power to ordinary people. In Europe, rival nations fought a devastating war from 1914 to 1918, shattering old beliefs about how societies should be run. In Russia, Communist revolutionaries overthrew the government in 1917. Then, from 1924 to 1939, brutal Communist dictator Stalin reorganized the country in a series of Five Year Plans.

Women munitions workers

While men were away fighting during World War I, women took over many of their jobs. These included heavy, dirty tasks, such as making weapons and driving lorries, that people had considered unsuitable for women until then. Women also served as volunteer nurses, sometimes in dangerous war-zones.

World War I

By 1900, the strongest European nations – Britain, Germany and France – were jealous of each other's industrial wealth, and envied each other's colonies overseas. They also quarrelled over the future of Serbia and other Balkan states. In 1914, war broke out between them. Germany, Austria–Hungary and Turkey fought against Britain, Russia and France. Other European nations, plus the USA, Canada, Australia, New Zealand and South Africa, soon joined in. Fighting lasted until 1918, when Germany surrendered.

The outbreak of the 1914–18 war was marked by massive troop movements, as British and French armies hurried to stop the Germans reaching the Channel coast. Both sides met face to face in Belgium and northern France. They dug lines of trenches (deep, narrow holes in the ground) to shelter their troops from cannon and machine-gun fire. The opposing armies remained in their trenches, gaining – or losing – very little territory, for the next four years

Russian Revolution

Many Russians hated their government, headed by Tsar Nicholas II. They thought him cruel, unfair and foolish. In 1917, he was overthrown by protesters called Bolsheviks. They were members of the Communist Party, led by a writer called Lenin. The Bolsheviks executed the Tsar and his family and took land away from rich nobles. After three years' civil war, the Communists controlled all Russia. They gave it a new name – the USSR (Union of Soviet Socialist Republics).

CHAIRMAN MAO

The last Chinese emperor was forced out of power in 1912. After that, there were many quarrels between rivals for the Chinese government. From 1916 to 1938 there were civil wars. In 1948, the Communists took control of China, led by Mao Zhedong (1893 – 1976). He made ambitious plans to modernize China. Today, Mao is often criticized, because his plans caused hardship for many Chinese people.

Irish nationalists confront British soldiers during the Easter Rising of 1916.

Easter Rising

Ireland had been ruled by Britain for centuries. In 1912, the British government said it would let Ireland have 'Home Rule' – its own parliament for making decisions about purely Irish affairs. But the majority of people living in the north of Ireland did not want to break away from mainland Britain; in the south, the majority wanted complete independence. At Easter 1916, about 1600 anti-British rebels seized important buildings in Dublin, and declared an Irish Republic. They were defeated by the British, and their leaders were shot. There were many more years of fighting and negotiations before the southern part of Ireland became an independent nation in 1937.

Many poor Spanish farmers supported the Republicans during the Civil War. They became guerrillas, hiding in wild countryside to attack Fascist soldiers, and creeping out at night to raid Fascist camps and weapons stores

Spanish Civil War

In 1936, civil war broke out in Spain. It was fought between Republicans (who wanted the people to have the right to choose the government) and Fascists (who supported a dictator who would keep citizens firmly under control). Young people from all over Europe travelled to Spain to fight for the Republicans, but many European governments supported the Fascists. The Fascist leader, General Franco, became ruler of Spain in 1939, and stayed in power until 1975. The Spanish Civil War saw the first-ever bombing raid from the air on unarmed civilians, at the Republican town of Guernica in 1938.

MAKE FLANDERS POPPIES

In many countries, red poppies have become a symbol of remembrance. They honour the millions of young soldiers who died in Flanders (present-day Belgium) in the 1914–18 war. To make Flanders poppies, cut thin strips of black paper about 10 x 2.5 cm. Make fringes along one long edge. Wind each strip round one end of a cork; fasten with sticky tape. Wrap a length of wire in green sticky tape, leaving 2.5 cm bare at one end. Push bare end of wire into cork. Cut 6 petals (about 10 x 10 cm) out of red paper. Use sticky tape to fasten petals to cork.

FAST-CHANGING WORLD

SINCE THE BEGINNING of the twentieth century, the world has changed more quickly than ever before. European empires in Africa and Asia have disappeared, and new independent nations have taken their place. New scientific knowledge has allowed people to reach the Moon and to find out more about the secrets of life on Earth. New medical discoveries have saved millions of lives. Fast cars and planes make it easy to travel long distances; telephones and televisions send information rapidly all round the world. But all this progress has brought new problems, such as overcrowding and pollution. Sadly, there is still a vast gap in living standards between rich and poor people. And many wars are still being fought.

World War II

In 1939, Hitler (see below) sent armies to invade Czechoslovakia and Poland; Britain, France and Russia decided to help the Czech and Polish people defend their lands. This marked the beginning of World War II. Italy and Japan allied with Hitler; Canada, Australia, New Zealand, South Africa and the USA joined Britain to fight against him. The war soon spread to British colonies in the Far East, and to China and the islands of the Pacific Ocean. Fighting continued until 1945. During the whole course of the war, over 15 million troops and at least 20 million civilians were killed.

From riches to rags

'Stocks' are shares of businesses. They can be bought and sold, and are often very valuable. In a 'crash', the value of stocks falls rapidly; they can become almost worthless. In 1929, the US stock market 'crashed'. Unemployment and poverty followed, in Europe as well as America. Charities ran soup-kitchens, and governments offered welfare payments, but throughout the 1930s, many families went cold and hungry.

Civilians under attack

The first powered flight took place in 1903. After that, engineers began to design many new and better aircraft. Because of these planes, World War II was the first in which civilians faced mass attacks from the air. Whole cities were flattened by bomb-blasts, or destroyed in 'firestorms'. Mass bombings were designed to cause panic and fear among ordinary people, and to force their leaders to surrender. But ordinary people on both sides of the war, as well as first-aid workers and fire-fighters, showed enormous courage. During raids, they hid in underground bomb-shelters – or under their kitchen tables. When the danger was past, they lived as best they could among the ruins.

HITLER

Austrian-born Adolf Hitler (1889-1945) became Chancellor (head) of the German government in 1933. He was leader of the extreme right-wing Nazi political party and had two aims: to make Germany the strongest nation in the world, and to get rid of all Jewish people and other minority groups. In 1934 he began to persecute all the Jews in Germany. They had to give up their jobs and businesses and wear special badges on their clothes. Later, he sent them to concentration camps (appalling prisons) where about 6 million died. When Germany was defeated in 1945, Hitler killed himself to avoid being captured and put on trial for his war crimes.

GANDHI

Mohandas Gandhi (1869–1948) devoted his life to ending British rule in India. He was a deeply religious man, who followed the Hindu faith, and a shrewd and intelligent politician. He won the support of millions of ordinary people in India, and led them on non-violent protest marches. After over 20 years of these campaigns, India finally became independent in 1947. Gandhi was shot dead the next year, by an Indian who disapproved of his support for religious toleration. He was given the name 'Mahatma' (Great Soul).

Atom bomb

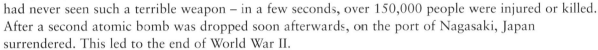

The first atomic bomb exploded over the city of Hiroshima, in Japan, on 6 August 1945. It was dropped by the USA. The world had never seen such a terrible weapon – in a few seconds, over 150,000 people were injured or killed. After a second atomic bomb was dropped soon afterwards, on the port of Nagasaki, Japan surrendered. This led to the end of World War II.

Fall of the Berlin Wall

After 1945 a dangerous tension developed between the capitalist USA and communist USSR. This was the 'Cold War'. Nations all round the world took sides. In 1961, a wall was built through Berlin in Germany to divide capitalist Western Europe from the communist East. The wall came down in 1989, when the communists lost control of the USSR, and the Cold War ended.

Space exploration

During the 1950s and 1960s, the USA and the USSR made astonishing advances in rocket technology and space exploration. In 1957, the USSR launched the first space satellite, and in 1961, sent the first person into space. The USA landed the first person on the Moon. American astronaut Neil Armstrong took his historic step on to the Moon's surface on 20 July 1969.

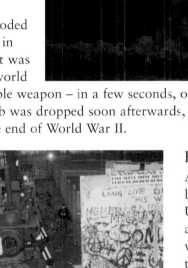

Russia's Mir space station

Computers and communications

The world's first computers were invented for army use during World War II. They were huge (the size of rooms) and very slow. Today, computers fly aircraft, control factories, and store vast amounts of data.

When linked by telephones to the Internet, they allow people all round the world to communicate with each other and share information.

During the 1990s more people than ever owned PCs (personal computers).

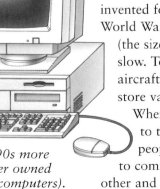

THE SPACE RACE

- 1957 First satellite in space (USSR).
- 1961 First man in space (USSR).
- 1969 First landing on the Moon (USA).
- 1981 First Space Shuttle flight (USA).
- 1986 First Mir Space Station (USSR).

INDEX

ACKNOWLEDGEMENTS

The publishers wish to thank the following artists who have contributed to this book:

Vanessa Card; James Field; Sally Holmes; Richard Hook; John James; Roger Payne; Mark Peppe; Terry Riley; Martin Salisbury; Peter Sarson; Roger Smith; Sue Stitt; Stephen Sweet; Michael Welply; Mike White

The publishers wish to thank the following for supplying photographs for this book:

Page 10 (C/L) Dover Publications; 11 (T/L) Mary Evans Picture Library; 17 (T/L) AKG Photo London; 18 (B/L) Freer Gallery of Art/E.T.Archive; 19 (C/R) AKG London; 31 (T/L) AKG London; 34 (T/R) AKG Photo London; 37 (C) AP/AKG London

All other photographs from Miles Kelly archives.